10659246

Lost AND Found

The Guide to Finding Family, Friends, and Loved Ones

Troy Dunn

MyFamily.com™

SOCIAL SCIENCES DEPARTMENT
BIRMINGHAM PUBLIC LIBRARY
2100 PARK PLACE
BIRMINGHAM, ALABAMA 35203

Library of Congress Cataloging-in-Publication Data

Dunn, Troy.
Lost and found : the guide to finding family, friends, and loved ones
/ Troy Dunn.
    p. cm.
  ISBN 1-59331-028-5 (pbk. : alk. paper)
  1. Missing persons—Investigation. I. Title.
  HV6762.A3D86 2003
  363.2'336—dc21

                                                    2003003665

Copyright © 2003 MyFamily.com, Inc.

P.O. Box 990
Orem, Utah 84059
www.myfamily.com

All Rights Reserved.

All brand and product names are trademarks or
registered trademarks of their respective companies.

Unless requested by them, the names of individuals
have been changed to protect their identity.

No part of this publication may be reproduced in any form
without written permission of the publisher, except by a reviewer,
who may quote brief passages for review.

First Printing 2003
10 9 8 7 6 5 4 3 2 1

Printed in the United States of America.

Lost AND Found

**The Guide to Finding
Family, Friends, and Loved Ones**

Introduction

Welcome to the MyFamily.com People Finder search and reunion guide. This book offers the information you need to find family and friends around the world.

Your guide along the way to discovery will be reunion specialist Troy Dunn. For the last decade, Troy has reunited thousands of loved ones worldwide utilizing the techniques discussed in this book. Some of his most memorable reunions have even been shared on national television in front of millions of viewers.

I remember the day a seventy-year-old woman named Kate Davis asked if I could help fill a void in her family that had been growing for twenty-three years. She told me about a thin, little girl with big, brown eyes named Addie. I could hear the emotion in Kate's voice as she told me how Addie had captured the Davis family's affection when Addie was their foster child more than twenty years earlier. Addie had lived with the Davis family for five years—much longer than the usual foster home placement. Kate, her husband, Linwood, and their two daughters, Hilary and Kris, all thought of Addie as a member of their family. They sent me photocopies of family portraits where Addie sat beside the two girls as if she'd always been their sister.

Yet, as soon as county officials realized the Davises had become attached to Addie and wanted to adopt her, she was transferred to another home. "The only reason I let them take her out of my house was that they told me she was going to live with her brother. That was the one thing I couldn't give her—her roots," Kate said tearfully. "And they said she would get counseling to help her heal from past abuse. There were no counseling services available in our small town."

Kate's voice turned wistful as she related a vivid memory from the first night Addie came to their home. At first, Addie suffered from both malnutrition and psychological problems. "Her previous foster family thought she was mentally challenged because she wouldn't talk," Kate said. "They wouldn't allow her to sit at the kitchen table. She was used to sitting on the floor and receiving scraps from their plates. When we all sat down to eat that first night, she sat under the table. My daughter, Kris, took her plate and sat under the table with Addie. It was the beginning of a wonderful friendship. Addie fit into our family immediately."

Addie blossomed in the Davis home and was soon talking, running, and playing like the other two girls. She enjoyed playing with her Barbie® doll, attending birthday parties, and going on summer vacations. When the social worker took her away, it was as if someone had left a hole in the Davis family. "They told us they would let Addie call us the first night, so we thought we might be able to stay in touch by phone. But she never called. When I asked for a phone number to call her, the social worker said it was legally against county policy to give it to me."

Although they never heard from Addie again, the Davis Family couldn't forget her and longed for the days when she had been part of their family. "We kept hoping we'd run into her on the street or see her somewhere. We didn't want to cause trouble. We just always felt like she was missing from our lives."

After twenty-three years, Kate's daughters contacted me for help in locating Addie. They could not have chosen a better surprise for Kate. "Asking you to find our Addie is their birthday present to me."

Like so many of the stories I hear every day, Kate's story touched my heart. Being a father of six, I can only imagine the pain of being separated from one of my children and longing to see that familiar, much-loved face once again. Wanting to help Kate and her family as quickly as possible, I pursued a search for Addie. I followed through with techniques I've used to reunite thousands of families around the world. Because these research methods are so effective, I didn't have to wait long to find answers.

Happily, we were able to discover that Addie Randall is now a successful, happy mother of four, who still considers herself to be the Davis's child. The most exciting part was that she had been looking for them, too. Through both hard and happy times in her life, she had held onto the memories and values that the Davis family had instilled in her at a young age.

"I never gave up hope of seeing them again," she told me. "I wanted to thank them one more time." She'd actually been looking for them by searching old phone books and consulting missing persons agencies. "I was so glad they wanted to hear from me," said Addie. "I never stopped thinking of them, and I hoped they didn't forget the good times we spent together."

When I brought Addie out on a television stage, tears flowed on everyone's faces—including mine. And I saw something that was much more obvious in person than in pictures. Addie really did share a family resemblance with the Davis family—she looked like she belonged.

"It was a miracle you found her after all those years," Kate said tearfully, recalling her first sight of the young woman who had been in her heart all that time. "I would recognize her anywhere. She looks exactly the same." Addie and the Davis family soon discovered that the bond between them was as firm as ever. Besides gaining a daughter, Kate was thrilled to become a grandmother for the first time by adding Addie's four children to her family.

It was another wonderful reunion. I can't tell you how great it feels to help patch the world back together, one family at a time.

My first search was for a missing person in my own family. My mother, grandmother, and brother are all adoptees—which means that adoption touches three generations of my family. I know personally how wonderful adoption can be, and I also understand the mysteries it creates. After my own family experienced reunions with lost family members, I dedicated my life to helping others who were searching for answers to a lifetime of questions. As I continued to work with adoptees and birth parents, I realized that these are powerful techniques that can also be used to find anyone who is missing. I will be sharing those techniques with you in this book.

If you are among the millions of people who are looking for someone from your past, you are about to embark on an exciting journey. Perhaps your search is one of the "big five" most common search categories—adoptee, birth parent, lost love, old friend, or military buddy. Or you may be searching for a past co-worker, former neighbor, childhood friend, or anyone else who lingers in your memory. These pages contain the strategies and information you will need to complete your search as quickly and simply as possible. Your reunion day is closer than you think!

Preparing for a Search

▼

*T*here has never been a better time to conduct a search for a lost loved one. Your likelihood of success is greater than ever for several reasons.

- Technological advances have put a wealth of information at your fingertips. For example, the Internet has brought a vast array of informational resources within your reach. From databases to websites to chat rooms, access to millions of relevant pieces of information is now yours in just minutes from the convenience of your desk.

- Access to public records has never been so broad. Along with the advent of the Internet, public records are now increasingly accessible and are often available online.

- With so many people conducting searches, the chance for a match is much greater. Increasing accessibility to information and rising interest in family history and searching for lost loved ones has resulted in increased networking among people who are searching. Many people who are searching for information and seeking a connection with their loved ones are also willing to share their knowledge and information with others.

- In the case of adoption searches, the idea of searching for a birth family has gained social acceptance. While many people once declined to speak publicly about adoption, they now discuss their adoption experiences openly. They join support groups—both online and offline. Those separated from loved ones and seeking to reconnect often chat together on the Internet, and are willing to share their feelings, search techniques, and the information they discover.

Because there are more search tools, techniques, and resources available now than ever before, your likelihood of success increases as you become familiar with the two methods of searching: online and offline. A proper mix of these methods will increase your chance of success. It's impossible to predict where and how you will find the one or more pieces of information that will solve the mystery of your search. For this reason, search in as many ways and as many places as you can. A variety of search efforts and sources will make you more likely to accomplish your goal and bring about the reunion you long to have.

Online Searching

Searching on the Internet offers you quick access to information when the record you need is available. The Internet opens its vast resources to you at the click of a button. It's possible to search ten or more websites within an hour—all without leaving your desk.

Lower cost is another advantage inherent in online searching. For example, in the most basic form of offline search, if you pick up your phone and dial directory assistance, the operator will provide two phone numbers for a cost nearly one dollar each. Also, you are required to make a separate call for each state. It's not possible to make a single request such as, "I'd like the number of Lynne Sorensen in San Francisco, California, and Lynne Sorensen in Schenectady, New York." Also, it's not possible to add that you are searching for a Lynne Sorensen between the ages of thirty-five and fifty-five, or that the Lynne Sorensen you are seeking is Hispanic.

Instead, for a nominal fee you can use the MyFamily.com People Finder <http://reunite.myfamily.com/> to seek instant information on Lynne Sorensen that is qualified by age, date, and location. The MyFamily.com People Finder also offers unlimited searching for ninety days. Within that time period, it's possible to search for Lynne Sorensen as well as other people you may be seeking.

If you find that you would like to receive still more information about a person, you can purchase a Detailed Report. Among the information this service can provide are the names that the person you are looking for uses, current and previous addresses and phone numbers for the person, and names and addresses of possible relatives and neighbors of the person at each of the addresses listed for them.

There are also many great opportunities to network and collaborate when searching online. More than 15 million people log on to the Internet each month looking for information regarding loved ones and acquaintances. Ten million of these people visit the MyFamily.com network of websites. (These message boards can be accessed at <www.ancestry.com> and <www.familyhistory. com>.)

The Internet connects a multitude of people in a myriad of ways. For example, the MyFamily.com message board network offers you the chance to communicate with others who are searching for, or who already have a connection with or information about, the person you are seeking. By finding a message board dedicated to the last name of the person you seek, you may find a connection—or at least information that leads to a subsequent connection.

More than 10 million messages have been posted on the MyFamily.com message board network. By posting on a message board, you can solicit the free and often helpful assistance of others who post. I recall a letter someone wrote to me about a reunion that came about as a direct result of a message board post. She wrote:

> *I was raised primarily by my mother because I never knew my birth father. They separated before I was born. After my birth, my mother married my stepfather and for most of my life he was the only father I knew. I often asked my mother and grandmother about my birth father but no one would tell me anything. What little I knew about him I read on my birth certificate.*

After my mother's death in 1994 I began searching for my birth father. Sadly, I found out that he had died in 1970 in a mining accident. A friend of mine helped me obtain a death certificate. With his help I was also able to locate several family members on my father's side in the little town of Ameagle, West Virginia. I was able to contact my father's brother, Barney, and he sent me pictures of my father. I was more than forty years old before I saw my father's face.

After finding the few relatives and seeing my father's face I was all the more determined to find additional family members. In December of last year with the help of my husband I started a family webpage and began using Ancestry.com to help me research my family name. I posted several messages on the surname message boards in hopes that someone else was also looking for information on my family.

I located my father's gravesite in Montana and my husband, son, and I went there so that I could pay my respects to the man I never knew but who had given me life. I wrote him a letter the night before and attached pictures of myself and my children. As I knelt by his grave and delivered the letter I cried at the thought that he and I had never had the chance to get to know one another.

When we got back home there was an e-mail from a man who was kind enough to send me an address for the daughter of my father. I was so excited that I wrote to her right away.

On the Stover Surname message board at Ancestry.com you will find a posting from my sister, Jenny Pruitt, proclaiming that we have found each other at last. She told me that she had been looking for me for many years.

Jenny and I have started corresponding and we met for the first time in April of this year. We have so much in common and have built a wonderful family bond. Although this sounds like the end of our story, it isn't. Jenny and I continue to use the message boards to try and locate more family members. In the past year we have located many cousins that we either didn't know we had or, in Jenny's case, had lost touch with.

Ancestry.com message boards have been a true blessing for me and Jenny. I was raised as an only child until the age of fourteen when my sister, Ellen, was born. I left home two years later. My mother and stepfather are both dead. I have no grandparents and until recently had no nieces, nephews, or cousins. I was afraid that I would die never knowing *my father or his family. I now have a sister, two brothers, two nephews, a niece, tons of cousins, aunts and uncles.*

Along with message boards, there are many websites you can consult. For example, you can simply put the name of person you are seeking in a search engine, such as Google, and find information that way. At the end of this book there is a list of many other online resources to consider. Your reunion could be just a click away!

Offline Searching

Every search is different. Right now you are in a unique situation, looking for a unique person. Your search is an adventure like no other pursuit in life. You may feel as though you are a detective, seeking clues and researching information. To search successfully, you need to be persistent, patient, and creative. You must turn over every informational "stone," remembering that no piece of information is too small and nothing is insignificant.

You will probably want to combine your online search with offline researching. There is an abundance of information available offline. People have achieved success through offline searches for years. It's often effective to combine both methods of searching in your efforts. You may find that a combination of online and offline searching leads you ever closer until you find the person you are seeking.

Call and Write

The telephone and the letter have been the primary ways of seeking information and keeping in contact for many years. Before the Internet, making a phone call or writing a letter were the quickest ways of connecting with another person. Searching online as well as seeking information by phone and letter will maximize your chance of success and will lead you to important avenues of information.

Libraries and Archives

Libraries and archives offer a wealth of resources and reference materials through which you may acquire information relating to the person you are seeking. Beginning with birth and continuing throughout our lives, almost all of our experiences and activities are recorded in some manner, whether we realize it or not. Census records (1930 and earlier), military records,

newspaper archives, and city directories are among the types of records available through libraries and archives. Plan to call ahead or check the institution's website to find out what types of records are available. The resources available in libraries and archives open up countless avenues for tracing the person you are seeking.

Talk to People

Searching for a lost loved one is not an exact science. It's not possible to guarantee that you will find the answers if you call a certain person or consult a particular website. Offline searching may be the place where you rely on your own instincts. You might get a feeling that if you meet with a particular man in person, he might happen to think of the information you need. You may feel that if you explain your situation by phone—while gauging the other person's reaction—you will be more likely to achieve results. With all the capabilities of the Web, it can't replace human contact. On some occasions, you may be more likely to find the information you need if you actually talk to someone by phone or meet them face to face. Or you may uncover a physical copy of a document that hasn't been posted on the Web. Be open to the possibilities of all types of information-gathering in your search.

Keep a Positive Search Attitude

To search successfully it helps to be persistent, patient, and creative. Remember that your search is a process of elimination. When your search yields a document or website that contains no new information, you are still one step closer to your reunion. You've eliminated one more possibility and narrowed your search effectively. With determination and attention to detail, you'll eventually find your person.

Plan to Organize

In order to find anyone, the first thing you need to do is to get, and stay, organized. You must keep accurate records. You will undoubtedly come into contact with people, documents, and bits of information that may seem irrelevant to the search. Keep track of every detail. Nothing is too trivial to save. There may come a time when one of these unimportant details turns out to be the missing piece you need to put everything together.

Don't leave original letters or documents lying around your desk. As soon as you get a letter or a document, copy it and put the original in a safe place where it can't be damaged or lost. Placing it in a safe deposit box is ideal. Now, with your original safely locked up, you can use the "working copy" you made in any way that makes the most sense to you. You can put the working copy in the filing cabinet or in your desk; you can index the document in your search workspace, or add the information to your notebooks—anything you want, because you'll never lose the original.

Being organized can be tedious, and it can be annoying at times. But it's the only way you'll be successful in your search. If you're serious about finding this person, get serious about organization.

Decide on a Filing System

Always make working copies of any information you find. If you are searching online and discover information on a website, print out two copies—one for your permanent files and another working copy to file in a notebook with pockets for loose papers. An expandable file will also work if you are printing a significant number of documents off the Web. Bookmark the site so you can refer to it again; you may find additional information in a second search. It's also helpful to bookmark sites you don't have time to explore at the moment, but that might prove useful later on.

Organize your bookmarks and favorite websites into folders, by topic. Also, the default website names may be clear now, but when you go back to scan your list of bookmarks, you may forget which site does what. Renaming the link reference can help you keep things straight.

Source and Document Checklist for _____
(name of person)

Personal and Family Memorabilia

Category/Item	Source of Information	Date Requested	Date Received
list of my personal memories			
interviews with family members			
photographs, scrapbooks			
family records			
medical or legal records			

Public Resources

Category/Item	Source of Information	Date Requested	Date Received
Library of Congress			
National Archives			
local libraries			
historical libraries			
genealogical societies			
state and federal census bureaus			
newspapers			

Download a copy of this form at <http://reunite.myfamily.com/forms>.

Use a Source Document Checklist

The source and document checklist, shown above, will help you keep track of documents you have requested and received. This list also provides a useful outline of sources you have explored, and options to consider when a particular avenue seems exhausted. You may want to consider copying the list so that you can keep it with other activity logs rather than writing in this book.

The following is a quick explanation of the columns in the source and document checklist.

Category/item—The average person living in the United States has participated in many activities that led agencies and organizations to generate documents containing information about him or her. Finding any one of these documents may give you a clue as to where that person is now or may lead you to the name of a person with additional information about your search.

Source of information—This is the agency, department, church, school, or the person from whom you received the information.

Date requested—Lists the date you wrote the letter or e-mail requesting information. Reviewing the list of letters you have written may remind you to follow up on previously submitted requests if you have not received a reply within six weeks.

Date received—This is where you list the date you received a letter, an e-mail reply, or a document.

Starting Your Search

*T*he Internet is a vast source of information that changes rapidly, and it will be a critical component of your search. Perhaps you already use the Internet daily, or maybe you've never touched a computer in your life. If you don't have a computer and/or Internet connection at home, you should be able to find one at a public library, community college, or university in your area. If none of those institutions has a public hookup, inquire at the nearest computer store. Many copy centers and computer service stores will provide access to the Internet.

Initial Internet Search

Don't let computer shyness deter you from giving the Internet a try in the course of your search. However, if you have no Internet experience, you should ask someone familiar with computers to give you a few quick lessons about the World Wide Web before you follow the instructions in this book. I won't take the time and space to discuss Internet basics here, but I will make a few general observations.

First of all, no single authority controls or regulates the Internet, and any person with a little computer knowledge can create a website. While this democratic approach gives Internet users access to incredible amounts of information, the free-for-all nature of the medium has also provided new arenas for scams and con artists. Most sites are completely credible, just as most businesses on the city streets are trustworthy. However, you should maintain a healthy degree of skepticism about claims made online. If it sounds too good to be true, be cautious. When giving out personal information online, be sure you have checked a site's credentials. Feel free to explore—just use common sense.

Second, be aware that the Internet is continually evolving. Since the publication of this book, some sites listed here may have moved to new locations. (Often when a site moves, the old site will list a forwarding address; but sometimes it won't, and you'll need to use a search engine such as <www.google.com> to track the site down at its new locale.) Some sites in the book may not exist any more; perhaps the people maintaining them could no longer afford to do so, or they may have moved on to other projects. And, of course, new and better sites may have come online after this book was printed.

As you pursue your search and surf the Internet, you should get in the habit of "bookmarking" sites. This is most helpful when you find sites you don't have time to explore at the moment, but that might be useful later on. If you don't bookmark them (or write down their addresses) you might not be able to find them again! It will also help to name the bookmark and keep similar bookmarks in the same folders. This will save you the frustration of having a number of bookmarks and being unable to remember why you marked them.

The great advantage to online searching is that you'll be off to a quicker start; searching from your home computer is much easier and faster than traveling to many libraries or making lots of phone calls. If you don't own a computer yet, you almost certainly would save money on your search by buying a computer because online searching saves so much time and money. Rather than driving to offices, or flying to another state or country to research a particular surname, or traveling to a cemetery to read names engraved on tombstones, you are able to sit at your computer in the privacy of your home and study records from around the world. For example, there are 1.7 billion names on the Ancestry.com site. It would require a huge facility to store physical copies of that many records, yet they are available at any time on your computer screen. Furthermore, access to information about most public records in every state in America is now available on the Web. Finding such information online is much faster than driving to every government office to seek out physical copies of the records.

Sites that I recommend are reviewed and approved by licensed investigators and certified researchers. The following guidelines will be useful to you in evaluating new sites.

- Information must be current and accurate. If you read through the text of the site without finding any dates or references from the current year, you may not be dealing with a frequently updated site.
- The site must be easy to navigate and understand.
- The site must not have any data, tips, or suggestions that are illegal or unethical.
- The site should have a good mix of content and commerce. You're looking for sites that are more interested in providing information for a good cause than in selling a product or service.

White Pages

You will find numerous white-page services on the Internet. When using such a website there are a couple of things to keep in mind. First, to use such a service you should know, at least a last name and a state. This will help to narrow down the number of "hits" you need to sift through. Second, don't be discouraged if you can't find your missing person listed on any of the white pages. Not everyone, after all, is listed in a white-pages directory. You may at least be able to find people with the same surname as the person for whom you are looking. You can then use those people as a starting point in your search given the possibility that they are related.

Databases

You can also find databases on the Internet that bring directory (white-pages) information and public records together in one powerful and easy to use search. The MyFamily.com People Finder <http://reunite.myfamily.com/> is one such "super search." The People Finder accesses a wide range of data that is in the public record, such as: property ownership databases, DMV and voter information databases, business ownership databases, professional license files and direct marketing sources. Purchasing a basic People Finder report provides simple contact information. Where available, this data includes name, address, phone number, and age. Once you think you have found the person you are looking for you can purchase a detailed report that includes previous addresses for the person and contact information for possible relatives and neighbors.

Genealogical Sites

One of the most effective search methods in the private investigation world is to drop back a generation and start the search from there. Sometimes people search diligently for a living relative and forget to consider the wealth of information that is available through genealogical research. If, for example, you are searching for Troy Dunn of Tampa, Florida, and you happen to find an obituary for his great-grandmother, you will discover that the obituary mentions a nephew in Arizona, lists surviving family members in California and Texas, and even refers to Troy himself, in Florida. That single obituary has given you not only Troy's home state, but the names and locations of surviving relatives who may offer important information.

Ancestry.com provides access to the Social Security Death Index. It can be searched online for free at <www.ancestry.com/search/rectype/vital/

ssdi/main.htm>. Ancestry.com also offers message boards from family members who are often conducting searches themselves and also have information to share <www.ancestry.com/share/>.

You will find hundreds of genealogical sites online, but I will list some favorites here. My preference for these sites is based on several factors. First, they are well-maintained and their data is current. Second, these sites offer numerous resources. You can find a census, an obituary source, the Social Security Death Index, and many other helpful resources all within the same site by using its index. These sites are also user-friendly and easy to navigate.

- **www.ancestry.com**—Ancestry.com connects Internet users to the most comprehensive online genealogical resources available. The site offers access to hundreds of millions of records containing over 1.5 billion names. You can search by record type, locality, or simply view scanned images of original historical documents. The Internet's most popular destination for pursuing family history research, Ancestry.com allows you to

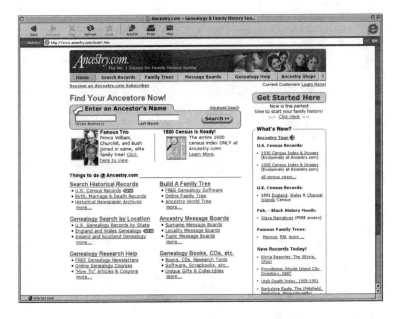

search some of the most coveted records available for family historians—including all available U.S. Census records (1790-1930). The site also offers extensive help and "getting-started" resources for those new to the pursuit of family history and free daily and weekly e-mail newsletters

- **www.rootsweb.com**—RootsWeb.com is the oldest and largest online community for genealogists. This free site contains extensive interactive guides and numerous research tools for tracing family histories. The site's WorldConnect Project contains more than 250 million ancestor names. The RootsWeb Surname List consists of a registry of over a million surnames submitted by more than 225,000 online genealogists. RootsWeb also boasts more than 25,000 mailing lists, and more than 10 million postings on 175,000 message boards. The site allows you to find people who do genealogical research on the particular name you are interested in. For example, if you want to know about the Peterson family of Wisconsin in the 1950s, you could enter those names and dates into this site, and the site would put you in touch with the Wisconsin-area Peterson family experts.

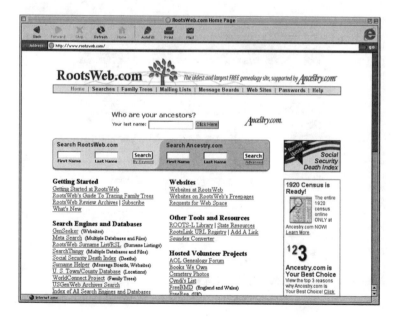

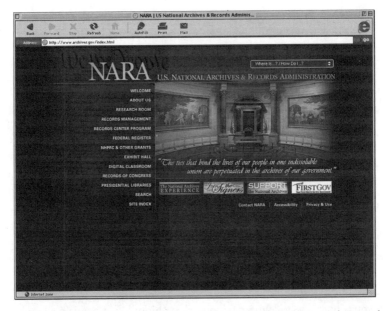

- **www.nara.gov**—This is the site of the National Archives and Records Administration (NARA). NARA is an independent federal agency that preserves the U.S. history by overseeing the management of all federal records. This site (and organization) makes governmental records available to the public. You'll find a wealth of historical information and research tools here.

- **www.cyndislist.com**—A no-cost jumping-off point for your online research, Cyndi's List is a categorized and cross-referenced index to genealogical resources on the Internet. With a comprehensive listing of almost 40,000 search sites, Cyndi's List is like a card catalog to the genealogical collection in the immense Internet library. It also offers a list of links that point you to genealogical research sites online. Cyndi's List is a great help for locating the sites that contain city directories, e-mail listings, postal zip codes, addresses, and many more worldwide resources.

- **http://newsdirectory.com**—NewsDirectory is your guide to all online English-language media. This free directory of newspapers, magazines, television stations, universities, visitor bureaus, governmental agencies, and more can help you get to where you want to go, or find sites you may not know about. NewsDirectory is a simple and fast site that can be used to access all the news and information you can handle.

Enlisting the Help of a Genealogist

Professional genealogists offer a variety of services. Most professionals conduct research on individual families and may specialize in geographic areas, ethnic groups, time periods, or particular records. They have experience analyzing lineages, planning research strategies, and evaluating evidence. Many also lecture, teach, publish, translate foreign language records, develop genealogical software, or provide consulting services (including on-site or in libraries and archives) for those who prefer to do their own family research. Others research medical projects (including family health histories) or legal cases; or conduct biographical and local history research for popular and academic writers, or document historic sites. Some professionals work independently; others are employed by genealogical business firms, libraries, or other organizations.

Contacting a Genealogist

If you contact a genealogist in person, ask for his or her credentials: education, professional affiliations, publications, foreign languages (if applicable), and access to records. For special projects, ask if the genealogist has had experience producing a completed family history in book format, conducting oral interviews with distant family members, or providing on-site photographs. If the research involves adoption, special ethnic origins, or uncommon problems, ask what experience the professional has in those specialties.

The Board for Certified Genealogists—Whenever possible, you'll want to enlist the help of a genealogist native to the area of your search. If this is not possible, you can locate a board-certified genealogist who may be able to assist you by contacting:

The Board for Certified Genealogists
P.O. Box 5816
Washington, DC 24403
www.bcgcertification.org

APG Directory—The Association of Professional Genealogists is an independent organization whose principal purpose is to support professional genealogists in all phases of their work: from the amateur genealogist wish-

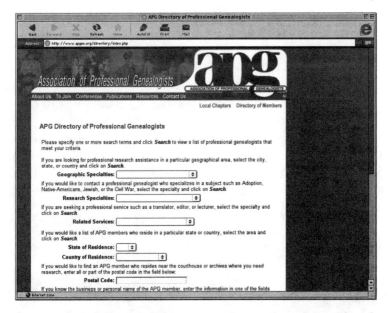

ing to turn knowledge and skill into a vocation, to the experienced professional seeking to exchange ideas with colleagues and to upgrade the profession as a whole. The association also seeks to protect the interest of those engaging in the services of the professional.

APG publishes a biennial paper directory. This volume is distributed free to public libraries and all members. A continually updated electronic directory is also available on the APG website at <www.apgen.org>. (It lists only those members who give permission to publish their information through this medium.)

Family History Centers

For decades, The Church of Jesus Christ of Latter-day Saints (the Mormons) has diligently gathered genealogical records from around the world and transferred them to microfilm. You can search for the church's nearest genealogy branch library (also called a Family History Center) through the Family History Library's website at <www.familysearch.org>. Records within a Family History Center include, but are not limited, vital record announcements, published directories, obituary indexes, census records, military records, church and parish records, birth indexes, and the Social Security Death Index. Furthermore, staff members at Family History Centers are both knowledgeable and helpful. There is no charge to access information at a Family History Center.

Registries

A registry is a database of people who are looking for someone. The idea behind the registry is simple. If you are looking for someone, it's possible that person is also looking for you. There are two types of registries: state reunion registries, which are owned and operated by a specific state, and privately owned operations. In most cases, signing up on a registry merely requires filling out an online or printed form. When both people sign up with the same registry, the registry links up their names and a match occurs. To get your feet wet, register with a site like Reunion Registry <http://www.reunionregistry.com>. Take a moment to look around this site to get a better idea of what a registry is all about.

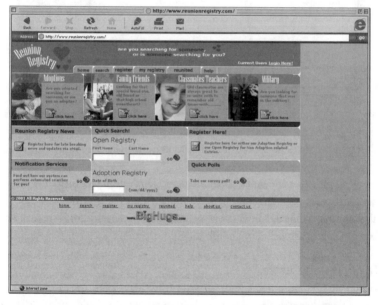

Keep in mind that signing up on a registry is a passive way of searching that requires mutual consent from both the searcher and the person being sought. Know up front that all registries are long shots. But if the person you are seeking has also decided to register, you have a 100 percent chance of not being rejected. Sign up on a few registries and then continue conducting an active, organized search through other avenues.

There are four things to consider when choosing a registry: size, location, longevity, and price.

- **Size**—Generally speaking, the more names in a registry, the greater your chance of success.

- **Location**—Most state-run registries are only open to people who were born or who relinquished a child in that state's borders. Adoptees and birth parents should strongly consider registering their information in both the state where the birth took place and the state where the adoption was finalized.

- **Longevity**—Since most state-sponsored registries are permanently established, this consideration is targeted primarily toward those that are privately owned. If you're considering joining a registry that charges a fee, call the Better Business Bureau in the town where the registry is located. Ask how long the registry has been in business and if it has a satisfactory business rating. The Better Business Bureau in your own city can give you the number for the BBB in the city where the registry is located.

- **Price**—It never hurts to enroll in a free reunion registry. While searching, you may encounter small private organizations who run small registries. Register if there is no charge. However, whenever a fee is involved, review the considerations above before making your decision. Some state-run registries charge a fee. It's been my experience that they're worth it, especially since increasing numbers of people are becoming aware of them. One last consideration is *how* the fee is structured. When there is an annual fee you will have to pay more money every year if you want to keep your name in their system. Once you are in a registry's computer system, it doesn't cost them anything to keep your name on file—so it doesn't make sense for you to pay a renewal fee every year.

I strongly encourage you to register with your appropriate state registries and with one international registry, like the Reunion Registry mentioned previously. Be aware that many privately owned reunion registries claim to be national or international. In reality, most of them cover only a specific geographic region and a few scattered registrations from outside that area. Do your homework to find the best registries for your particular search.

Expanding the Search

As you continue to pursue your search, you may find that it takes you to a variety of destinations that you weren't familiar with when your search began. You may learn that the person you are seeking is an accountant and you find yourself scouring websites that list members of accountant associations. You may discover that the person you are looking for is a published writer, and you may read his works online before you meet him in person. You may find the personal website belonging to the person you are seeking, and can get to know him or her online before you speak for the first time. Remember that both the Internet and offline search materials are constantly changing, and you could continue to gather new information online throughout your search.

Background Checks

Background checks are becoming routine, whether your subject is a potential employer, a nanny, a fiancé, a renter, or a birth parent. Many people, as they get close to finding someone, will want to know more about the person they're about to contact. What if you are looking for a lost love from high school? After you have found the person's city and address, you may suddenly find yourself nervous about making contact. If it's been a long time since you last saw the person you've been searching for, a background check could be in order.

Regarding background checks, the more information you can provide about the person you are seeking, the more information the results will contain. Be sure that all of the facts you supply to the background checker are accurate, especially with regard to spelling and dates.

I have found the website FullReport <www.fullreport.com> to be staffed by professional investigators who take great pride in their vast resources. They are able to check assets, liens, employment, education, professional licensing, aliases, and other sensitive areas.

Offline Searching

Just as your online search will likely widen to include a variety of destinations, your offline search and its results may lead you to seek information from previously unfamiliar sources as your search progresses. You may feel like a detective unearthing clues with each new discovery. You may find yourself writing to people or organizations whose names were unknown to you before your search began. Perhaps you will visit a state you never thought about beyond a school geography class. You might find a relative with a delightful accent, or reacquaint yourself with an old friend who seems like she hasn't changed a bit. Part of the excitement and intrigue of searching is that you don't know where it will lead you. Be open to the possibilities and use your ingenuity even as you pursue the traditional methods of offline searching like making phone calls and writing letters.

Phone Calls vs. Writing Letters

In making an initial contact, remember that if you choose to write a letter first, you can direct the course of the request more easily than if you make a phone call. You can take the time you need to word the request the way you want. You can state all of the facts without being interrupted or questioned.

On the other hand, a phone call is much quicker than a letter. If you don't receive an answer to a letter, a follow-up phone call can determine if the letter was ever received. If you have a simple, straightforward question that requires no detailed research or personal information such as—"Is this the department where the archives are housed?," or "Is non-identifying information available from this agency?"—a phone call may resolve your dilemma and help you decide whether to write a detailed request by letter.

Writing Letters

Whenever possible, make your first contact with an agency or organization in writing. This allows you to plan each question and statement carefully. It also doesn't give the one from whom you're requesting information the chance to quiz you with probing questions. The following are some basic guidelines you should follow whenever you request information by letter.

- Put yourself in the position of the person reading your letter. Anticipate that person's response. I recommend that your first requests be handwritten and informal to set the recipient at ease.

- If you're claiming urgent reasons such as a medical emergency or legal proceedings, request overnight or second-day delivery to reinforce the impression that your request is urgent. It also makes sense to include extra postage in your request to cover express return shipping.

- Never ramble. Don't give the recipient too much information. Use integrity and sincerity, but don't give your life history.

- Send a wallet-size color photo of yourself and your family (if you have one). The recipient will automatically attach a face to your request, which will make it personal.

- Be as accommodating as possible. Offer to pay any search and duplication fees. Use a money order rather than a personal check to pay fees. Send all letters with a self-addressed, stamped envelope to demonstrate your sincerity and encourage a timely response.

- Include two character references—one from a clergy member if possible.

- Notarize a letter or send a request by certified mail to make it seem more important and to catch the recipient's attention. Generally, a letter should be notarized when you
  a. want to prove that the contents of the letter are factual,
  b. need to verify that you are the person making the request,
  c. haven't received satisfactory cooperation in your previous attempts.
  Your bank or credit union will typically have a notary public on staff to notarize letters. Notaries can also be found in the yellow pages of your telephone directory. If you are a member of AAA, you may have free notary services available at the nearest office. Don't forget to make copies of these letters for your search planner after they have been notarized. Mailing a letter certified mail/return receipt requested is a good idea when sending important items such as certified documents and legal papers. It costs a little more, but you will have both written proof that your request was received as well as the signature of the person who accepted it. The postmaster will give you a receipt, which you should put in your search planner.

- Do not mention "adoption search" as a reason for your request unless it is absolutely necessary. Clerks may feel uncomfortable helping with an adoption search, which will lead them to prejudge your intentions and refuse to give you information they might otherwise routinely release. I use the term "genealogy search" in place of adoption search when making a request. The goals are the same in terms of information you are seeking, and following this rule can greatly increase your chances of success. You may want to say something like, "I am doing a family history research project. Since I was not raised by my biological family, I depend on people like you to help me find my roots."

- Include effective phrases in your letter, such as:
  "I'm an ordinary person who cannot afford costly private detectives or attorneys. I depend on your good faith and effort to help me. Please don't let me down."
  "A few moments of your time may unlock the door to my true bloodline. This will affect my happiness, and my family's, for a long time."
  "No clue is insignificant. Any help, however small, will be deeply appreciated."
  "Please go the extra mile for me. I'm depending on you."

Even though the officials receiving your letters may be somewhat conservative, they are nonetheless human and have emotions and a conscience. If your first correspondence is unsuccessful, keep trying different variations. Chances are good that you'll eventually get the information you need.

Making Phone Calls

Good telephone skills are essential to any successful search. The most valuable phone lesson is to learn when to use the phone and when to write first. Since a telephone call is a freeform, two-way exchange of information, it's anyone's guess what will happen once the conversation begins. Therefore, since a great deal depends on how you ask for the information you need, it is important to prepare yourself in advance (both mentally

and physically) for these contacts. By following the guidelines presented below, you will maintain control of each call and receive the maximum amount of information.

The Five Rules of Telephone Conversations

As you go about your search, you will find that the most successful phone calls are the ones that follow up on letters. During such telephone conversations, keep your conversation log handy (see below) so that you can take notes on the calls you make and the facts you receive. The following are some basic guidelines you should follow whenever you request information by phone.

- Before making a contact, prepare a detailed list of questions. Address every issue you want to cover. Decide the best order to ask these questions. Write your questions in a conversational tone, so they sound natural. Keep this list near you during the entire call. Obviously, there will be some give and take during the phone call, but keeping the list where you can see it will help you stay on track and help assure that the information you receive is complete.

- Rather than seeking a yes or no response, prepare open-ended questions so that you leave the other person plenty of opportunity to respond. For example, if you asked your mother, "Was my father in the military when you met him?" she might answer no. Don't insert information you know, or think you know, into the question. Here's an example of an open-ended question: "How did you meet my father?" Such open-ended questions lead to far more information and you won't restrict the answer with your own assumptions.

- With the prior permission of the person being interviewed, always record your phone conversations. As a conversation proceeds, it's easy to get caught up in the moment and forget to listen to what is being said. When this happens, you will miss important bits of information that would be lost forever if they aren't recorded. Once you play back the tape, chances are you will be surprised to discover details you didn't notice before. Equipment to record conversations is inexpensive and well worth the cost. In most cases, you will only need a basic tape recorder and a telephone pickup jack. A pickup jack is essentially a small suction cup that attaches to the receiver of your phone. A pickup jack is available at almost any electronics store for about five dollars.

• Don't ramble. Work hard to keep your talking to a minimum without seeming rude. Be friendly in order to build rapport with the person to whom you're talking, but try not to volunteer too much information (which is what will happen if you talk too much or feel the need to talk in order to fill a silence). The less a person thinks you know, the more cooperative that person will be.

• In an adoption search, unless you're in a situation where your call obviously relates to adoption, never mention the word "adoption" unless it's absolutely necessary. Phrases such as "doing a family genealogy" or "searching for family medical information" are very effective, whereas, "trying to locate my birth parents" only makes people nervous. Consider, too, that in not mentioning the word "adoption," you are respecting the privacy of your birth mother who may never have told anyone she placed a child for adoption. If you are a birth parent, you are respecting the privacy of your child, who may have been raised without knowing he or she is adopted. To respect privacy in the case of an adoption search, use sentences like "My family is researching our family genealogy, and we're trying to trace a few distant branches of our family," or "I am searching for family medical information. I would appreciate any information you may have."

Conversation Log

It is estimated that people remember less than half of what they see and only about one-third of what they hear. However, they remember more than seventy percent of what they both see and hear. That is why I strongly recommend keeping a conversation log and tape recording all telephone calls relating to your search (within the limits of the law).

A conversation log can be any notebook, tablet, or ring-binder with lined paper. Since you will be talking to many people and making valuable contacts during your search, it is vital to maintain an accurate log of all the telephone calls you make and receive. Each page of your conversation log serves as the record of a phone call. At the top of each page of the log, write the date and time of the call, the organization or person you spoke with, his or her name, (it is always important to get the full name of the person you are talking with, especially when dealing with a large organization), and his or her phone number.

On the rest of the page, note important details of each call. Was a particular individual helpful or unhelpful? Might he or she be a helpful resource in the future? Did you learn any personal details about this person? In many instances, remembering someone's name and referring to a previous conversation will make the person feel more comfortable with you the next time you call.

Any information you learn about the person you're looking for must be written in this log, too, so you'll remember who told you the information and when you obtained it. If there's a need to follow up with this person, note that as well.

It's important to take detailed notes along with recording. Why? Because if you forget a piece of information, you can track it in your notes, rather than listening to one or more entire tapes to find the information again. You can just flip through your conversation log and find the relevant fact, and then, after you know which conversation the fact came from, you can refer to the specific tape for details.

Correspondence Log

The correspondence log is like the conversation log; however, it only keeps track of the e-mails you send or letters you write. Any notebook will work for a correspondence log. Divide each page of your correspondence log by drawing a line down the middle. On the top left side, write "Correspondence." On the right side, write "Response."

At the top of each page on the correspondence side, write the date you sent or received each e-mail or letter, whom the correspondence was from or to, and the subject of the communication. On the "Response" side, write the date you received a response, or the date you sent a response.

On the rest of the page, make notes of any significant facts or details you learned as a result of this correspondence. Once again, this log is not meant to replace copies of the correspondence itself, which should be kept in both a working and a permanent file.

Library Log

Your library log will allow you to record important reference data such as online reference sources, page numbers, book titles, authors identification numbers and brief descriptions of vital information you find while researching in a library.

The library log can be any notebook that you'll take along to the library when you research. Across the top of each page in the notebook, write the name and location of the library you're visiting, the librarian's name, the date, the title of any database or reference book you found helpful, any Web addresses or reference numbers associated with that information source at the library, and the author or publisher of that reference. On the page itself, copy the useful information and Web address or page numbers where you found the information. Even if you make copies on the library copy machine, it is important to accurately list the source in the library log so that you can locate a piece of information easily rather than searching through the copies you've made from websites or reference books.

Search Maps

Your search will probably produce more documents, records, copies, and pieces of information than you expect. A search map will allow you to quickly identify which documents and websites contain the desired information.

A search map can be made from an 8.5" by 11" piece of paper. Down the length of the paper on the left side, list each document you have obtained. List the pieces of information contained on that document across the rest of the width of the paper.

As you find information online or receive a new document, make a new entry describing the particular information or listing contained in the document. Later, you'll be able to scan your search map quickly to find the information you're looking for. It will be a lot easier to locate records than to look through twenty or thirty documents and try to decipher the fine print on each one.

Search Strategies

▼

*T*here are some informational resources, such as libraries and archives, whose reference materials may be available online, offline, or both. Likewise, there are some types of information—such as newspapers and telephone directories—that may be available in either format. If a resource offers information in either hard copy or online, you may want to consider online searching first to save time, or to conduct a quicker initial search of many references. On the other hand, a combination of search methods may lead you to discover the information you are seeking. Sometimes, in browsing through a book, you may encounter a new topic or unfamiliar reference that you were previously unaware of, and therefore didn't know how to seek online.

Libraries

Your local library is an important resource in your search. Most reference librarians enjoy taking on a challenge and can help you sift through the maze of available information. Library materials will typically include a wide variety of reference sources. Online databases are a recent innovation that make a wealth of information available and offer a broad range of research materials.

Reference materials such as maps and cross-street directories, old telephone books, and voter registrations offer information that may help you locate the person you are seeking. Historic information such as family records and histories, microfilm of newspaper articles, obituaries, old voter registration records, and genealogical information may also be helpful.

Libraries are also a good source of a variety of professional directories. The American Library Directory of national, state, city, and county libraries lists libraries across the country. The *Guide to American Directories* lists directories published by all business and professional organizations. Professional directories list names and addresses of doctors, lawyers, organizations, colleges, universities, trade, alumni, and religious organizations. Another directory reference, *The Encyclopedia of Associations,* includes experts and organizations related to every topic imaginable—from the Lithuanian Catholic Priests League to the Horseless Carriage Club of America to the Organization for Collectors of Covered Bridge Postcards.

Don't be discouraged if some or all of your search must be conducted outside the county or state in which you live. Librarians have access to many of the documents or microfilm records you need through the interlibrary loan program. Specific family records and histories, for example, are often available through the Library of Congress in Washington, D.C. The loan program gives each library access to materials from other libraries across the country, including the Library of Congress. It typically takes two to four weeks to get information in this manner.

National and State Archives

The National Archives is a federal repository whose public records date back to the 1700s. It holds a wealth of information, including naturalization, military, census, and other family background records. There are twelve branches of this agency in addition to its national headquarters in Washington, D.C.

Some regional branches of the National Archives have certain types of records unique to their region. One can either call and inquire if a particular type of information or record is available at a regional branch or go to <www.archives.gov/facilities/index. html> for information about each regional archive. Criminal, civil, and bankruptcy court records are normally kept in the National Archives.

Each state also maintains its own state archives, where state, county, and local records are to be sent. City directories are sometimes housed in the state archives. *The Ancestry Family Historian's Address Book* (Ancestry, 2003) has a complete listing of national and state archives along with addresses of public libraries and genealogical societies.

Again, if you are contacting the National Archives or a state archives regarding an adoption search, it is best to say you are "researching your family tree."

Telephone Directories

The first place many people try to find someone is in the telephone book. Often, however, the person has moved, married, or has an unlisted number.

If you think you know the town where the person you are seeking lives, and you believe he or she has an unlisted number, simply call directory assistance and give the name. If directory assistance tells you there is no listing under that name, then the person you are looking for may not live in the town. You may be told that the number is unlisted and cannot be released. Either way, you will know whether or not the person you are seeking lives in the area.

Thanks to online searching, there are faster ways to get this information on a national basis. White-pages websites and other databases contain the names, addresses, and telephone numbers of ninety percent of the people in the United States.

Cross Street Directories

Cross street directories are valuable sources that allow you to locate a name and address from a telephone number and vice versa. They can be an excellent way to identify neighbors of the person for whom you are looking. Searching by address or phone number is also available on many websites.

Social Security Records

Since almost everyone has a social security number, it is likely that the Social Security Administration will have the employment records or the home

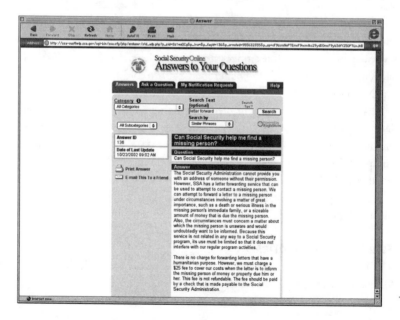

address of the person you are seeking—especially if that person is old enough to be receiving benefits.

While the SSA will not allow you to contact a person directly, it will forward mail to that person for "humanitarian purposes." This normally includes matters of medical urgency, legal proceedings, and estate settlement. Genealogical reasons are usually not considered to be sufficient cause and "adoption search" is always a sure candidate for rejection. If your request is accepted, the SSA will contact the individual, informing him that he is under no obligation to respond. But if he does, you will have made contact with the person you are looking for.

To contact the SSA, address your request to:
Social Security Administration
Letter Forwarding Service
Office of Central Records Operation
300 N. Greene St.
Baltimore, MD 21201
General Inquiry Number (800) 772-1213

Specific Searches

Adoption Search

*T*here are millions of adopted people in the United States today. Many of them are searching for their roots. Ninety percent of adoptees are placed in caring, happy homes, and ninety percent of reunions are favorable in that adoptees find answers.

While most genealogy could be compared to an archaeology dig, a process in which layer after layer of history is unearthed, adoptees need to

unpuzzle more personal mysteries—like where they got their green eyes or why their big toe is shorter than their second toe. The real reason adoptees search for their roots is to solve the dual identity they've lived with for so long. For some adoptees, it's as if they started their life on chapter two and the rest of the book doesn't quite make sense until they know what happened in chapter one.

Initial Information Report

If you are an adoptee, your search should begin with an initial information report. Buy a notebook and use it as a memory notebook. Plan to spend uninterrupted time answering the following questions from your own recollections. There will be time to refer to documents and interview family members later.

Don't be discouraged if you know very little about your birth family. It's unusual to know more than your own date and place of birth. The only source of knowledge for most adoptees is the information their adoptive parents gave them as they were growing up.

The two purposes of the memory log are to create a list of everyone who may know something about your adoption and to write down every shred of information you can remember. Be sure to include casual remarks you may have heard over the years. The important thing is to write down everything you remember.

Copy each of the following questions in your notebook, then write as much of an answer as you can manage, completely from your own memories.

- Was I named at birth? What was my original name?
- What have I heard about my birth parents?
- How old were they when I was born?
- Where was I born?
- What was the name of the adoption agency?
- What was the name of the doctor who delivered me?
- What are the names of every person I can remember who was involved in my adoption in any way?

Once you've done this, make copies of the Adoptee Family Interview Sheet (see example on page 38). Give a copy to every individual you can remember or who you have learned was involved in your adoption. Ask each of them to take time individually to fill in as many blanks as they can. By doing this independently rather than in a group, no one person's judgment or memories will override another's. After they've finished, go over each of their answers with them to the extent that you feel comfortable.

If you plan to tell your adoptive parents about your search, now is the time to share your information and your feelings. My experience has been that adoptive parents often feel uneasy about raising the issue of searching. They frequently decide early on to wait until the child asks before discussing the matter. But once the child makes his or her own decision to search, adoptive parents generally have a positive reaction to the search. Often, your adoptive parents will provide valuable support and you will become closer in the process.

Adoptive parents and other family members can be helpful in your search. Many times, they have been inadvertently exposed to documents that contain the names of your birth family. They may have even kept documents without realizing their significance.

Finally, fill out the Birth Family Tree (see page 39). This will give you an ongoing record of your search results and help you decide which direction to pursue in seeking additional information. You may discover that it is often

Adoptee Family Interview Sheet

Make copies of this form for every family member/friend who is going to be interviewed. Fill in every blank—if you don't know the answer use "unknown." Label answers that are known for certain with a star (*). Use this list as a basic guide and attach any questions of your own on the last page.

1. Exactly where was I born? _____

2. What was the name of the hospital? _____

3. Do you have a copy of my amended birth certificate? _____ Where is it? _____

4. Do you have a copy of my original birth certificate? _____ Where is it? _____

5. What were you told about my birth parents? _____

	Birth Mother	**Birth Father**
Names:		
Ages:		
Exact DOBs:		
Places of Birth:		
Nationalities:		
Education Levels:		
Religions:		
Military Service:		
Physical Descriptions:		
Marital Status:		
Other Children:		
Their Parents:		
Their Brothers/Sisters:		
Deaths in Family:		

Download a copy of this form at <http://reunite.myfamily.com/forms>.

easier to get detailed information about extended birth family members, such as aunts, grandparents, and siblings, than it is to get information about the birth parents themselves.

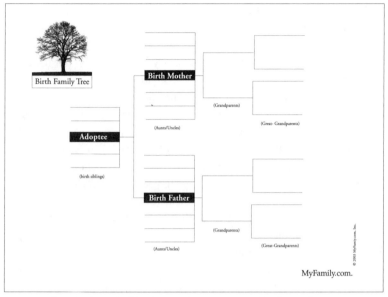

Birth Family Tree

Adoptee

(birth siblings)

Birth Mother

(Aunts/Uncles)

(Grandparents)

(Great- Grandparents)

Birth Father

(Aunts/Uncles)

(Grandparents)

(Great-Grandparents)

© 2003 MyFamily.com, Inc.

MyFamily.com.

Download a copy of this form at <http://reunite.myfamily.com/forms>.

Contacting Adoption Agencies

Your first contact with a state and or/private agency should be in writing. A carefully written letter gives you the opportunity to get a feel for how cooperative the agency will be. If you're an adoptee, your search typically begins by contacting the agency where you were adopted to ask for "non-identifying information." While providing non-identifying information is legal in every state, some adoption agencies or state organizations have established policies against supplying non-identifying information. Such policies are usually initiated because adoption agencies feel that their staff's time is limited and they cannot afford the time it takes to research and draft the non-identifying information document. Many agencies charge a nominal fee to provide non-identifying information.

Non-identifying information often provides more detail than the agency gives the adoptive parents. It might include the date the adoption was finalized, the number of siblings in the birth parents' families, hereditary health conditions, and nationality information. It's likely to also mention interests, physical appearance of the birth parents, and details about the adoption circumstances.

Laws differ from state to state, but most follow the general policy of withholding from an adoptee or birth parent any piece of information considered to be identifying. Basically, that means anything that could allow you to directly identify or locate someone. No agency will supply the full name or current address of a birth parent or adopted child.

Many states have moved toward opening adoption records and allowing adoptees to receive more complete birth information, typically the original birth certificate. "Open" records may also mean adoptees can access all the information in the adoption case file. Five states have "open" records, seven are "closed," and the remainder offer varying degrees of openness. Along with the official information that may be legally yours in the state where your adoption took place, you naturally want identifying information that will help facilitate your reunion. The suggestions that follow will help you as you seek this additional information.

Incidentally, most adoption agencies and related organizations do not consider military backgrounds as identifying information. As such, it's fairly easy to find out if the person you're looking for is or ever was in a branch of the service. Even if you don't have a name yet, knowing that your birth father or birth mother was in the military will give you a huge advantage in your search and will direct you to the military resources listed in another section of this book.

After sending your first letter to the adoption agency, you will receive some kind of reply. If the agency where you were adopted offers non-identifying information, request that valuable information. There may be a small fee of up to fifty dollars. Non-identifying information is often enlightening in itself and may offer clues that lead you further in your search for identifying information. For example, your non-identifying information may indicate that your birth mother had two brothers and one sister and that her father died of heart trouble when she was ten. Although such facts don't reveal her identity, they can be used to help confirm whether a person you find in your search is the actual person you are seeking.

Regardless of the type of reply you receive in your first letter to the adoption agency, use it as an opportunity to follow up and keep the dialogue open in your effort to find identifying information. I have found that many times people become so uncomfortable repeatedly saying no and being so obviously uncooperative that they actually want to find something positive they can tell you. Help them help you.

After your second or third letter, you may feel comfortable enough to follow up by phone. You may even have a person's name from the agency by now. Call that person and introduce yourself by saying, "I really appreciate the time and effort you've put into our correspondence. I wondered if I could take a minute of your time."

Be sure to make notes of any personal comments the person has made. For example, if you are working with a person—a woman, let's say—and she comments that she hasn't returned your call for a few days because she was out sick, the next time you talk to her, you might ask if she is feeling better. Your sincere concern for her will help develop a better working relationship between the two of you. It's much easier for the adoption agency employee to say no to a piece of paper than to a voice or a face; and it is much easier to say no to a stranger than to someone with whom you have a personal relationship.

I've found some techniques to be especially helpful when dealing with adoption agencies.

- Whenever you are denied specific information, request pieces of it. For example, if the agency won't tell you someone's name, ask for their initials. If they refuse to give you a specific date of birth, ask for the month or the time of year. These little bits of information are not a compromise of the person's duties to keep identifying information confidential, but they can help you immensely.

- Ask yes or no questions to pinpoint general information, such as "It would be really helpful to me if you could just give me the smallest start in the right direction. Nothing that's identifying, just a little piece of information. Okay? Please tell me…does the first initial of my mother's first name come before the letter M?" (Well…um…no, it doesn't come before M.") "Does it come after T?" ("Well, yes, it's after T…" "After W?" At this point, the person may say, "Look, we can't go over this name letter by letter all day long!" But at least you've narrowed down the first initial to a fairly small group.

These techniques can work equally well when talking with a doctor or attorney who was involved in the adoption. Be informal and non-threatening in your contacts and be patient. It may take several calls to build a relationship and get the information you need.

Online Resources for Adoption Searches

As you proceed in your search, you may be able to use some of the following websites. At the beginning of your quest, however, you may not even know the name of the person you are seeking. If that is the case, you will need to go to websites that are specifically oriented toward the adoption search. There are several good ones.

• **Cyndi's List**—www.cyndislist.com/adoption.html

This adoption link is from Cyndi's List, a genealogical site that includes a wide variety of links, references, and resources. This link provides a connection to dozens of other adoption links in the following categories:

General Resource Sites
Locality Specific Links
Mailing Lists, Newsgroups & Chat Resources
Professional Researchers, Volunteers & Other Research Services
Publications, Software & Supplies
Societies & Groups

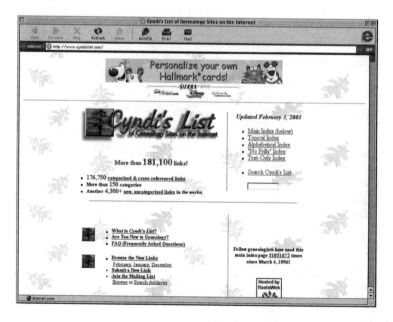

• **Adoptees Internet Mailing List**—www.aiml.org

AIML is an Internet mailing list. It provides a centralized e-mail address through which all adoptees who are AIML members can send e-mail to one another. Only active members are allowed to send and receive messages. This list is designed to be a place where adoptees can gather for advice in conducting a search and/or discussions of varied reunion outcomes. This e-mail exchange also encourages discussions of social, media, and legal issues related to adoption. Membership to AIML is restricted to legal adoptees and "adoptee-lites" only (adoptee-lites are people who were raised without one or both birth parents, but who were never legally adopted).

• **Sunflower Birthmom Support Page**—www.bmom.net

Alana, a birth mother, originated this mailing list as a support group for other birth mothers. She describes this site as a place where birth mothers can discuss feelings about giving children up, search efforts, reunion issues, and any other issue they wish to raise. Postings are sent to subscribers by e-mail. The site also includes a list of links designed to help in reunion search efforts. It also features a long list of online registries and a database link page.

• **The International Soundex Reunion Registry**—www.isrr.net

The International Soundex Reunion Registry is a system for matching persons who desire contact with their next of kin by birth. Adoptees who are eighteen years or older, birth parents, and adoptive parents of adoptees who are under eighteen years of age may register. When a registration is received, the information is computerized. If data matches and the ISRR registrar determines that a relationship exists, both parties are notified immediately. ISRR is a non-profit, tax-exempt corporation funded entirely by donations. There is no fee or cost for this service, although donations are encouraged. All contributions are tax-deductible. This registry does not perform a search or provide search advice. Registrants are held responsible for all information provided on their form and any documentation attached thereto. You can obtain a registration form online at <www.plumsite/isrr.com> or by sending a self-addressed stamped envelope to:

I.S.R.R.
P.O. Box 2312
Carson City, Nevada
89702-2312
(775) 882-7755

• **ReunionRegistry.com**—www.reunionregistry.com
The largest registry in the world with hundreds of thousands of sub-scribers from all fifty United States and more than 144 countries. Founded nearly a decade ago, ReunionRegistry.com was created as a free resource to assist friends and families in locating and reuniting with one another. To date, ReunionRegistry.com has facilitated hundreds of reunions.

• **Tina's Adoption Reform and Search Pages**—www.geocities.com/CapitolHill/9606/
Tina Musso, an adoptee who was reunited with her birth mother, created this site to help other adoptees in their searches for their birth families. Along with general advice about searching, the site includes state by state informa-tion regarding adoption records and registries, adoption facts and statistics, links to online databases, and book reviews.

Birth Parent Search

Most adoptees who are "search age" were adopted through an act of secrecy. When birth parents went through the process, they were told to go on with their lives and forget about the event. Very few can do that. If you are a birth mother, chances are you looked in every baby stroller you passed to see if a baby there looked like you or the baby's father. Birth parents usually have a hope or wish to meet their child again someday—not to step back into the child's life as mother and father, but rather to see that the child is healthy and happy and to put closure to the event. Some birth parents hope for a day when they will get a phone call or a letter in the mail. Others decide to take the initiative and begin the search themselves. Today, adoption reunions are more likely to take place than ever before. One out of fifty peo-ple is an adoptee, and sixty percent of birth parents and adopted children eventually meet.

Initial Information Report

As a birth parent, your search begins with an Initial Information Report. Fill out this log from your own memory. It's unusual at this stage to remember more than your child's date and place of birth and his or her birth name, if given. Typically, the only source of this information is your own memory, since most birth parents receive little or no documentation to show that the event even occurred.

The two purposes of this log are to create a list of everyone who may know something about your adoption and to write down every shred of information you can remember.

Answer the following questions:

- What was my name at the time of the birth?
- Where and when did the birth occur?
- What did I name my child?
- What was the name of the adoption agency?
- What was the name of the attorney involved?
- What was the name of the doctor involved?
- What is the name of each person I can remember who was involved in the adoption in any way? (Include the names of all doctors, hospitals, clergy members, lawyers, state or private agencies, and officials you can remember.)

Once you have done this, the next step is to make copies of the Birth Parent Family Interview (see following page) for every family member or friend named in your memory log. Do not contact any officials at this point. You will be able to contact them later, in the other ways suggested earlier in this book. Ask your family and friends to each fill in as many of the blanks as they can. After they've finished, go over each of their answers with them to the extent that you feel comfortable. Keep in mind that valuable information can often come from unlikely sources.

Online Resources
See the previous section for information on using the Internet to aid in your adoption search.

"Old Friend" Search
Elizabeth Christensen never forgot her friend, Pat Mason. As teenage girls in Texas, Pat and Elizabeth went everywhere together, from movies to baseball games to Elvis Presley concerts. They even shared getting into trouble. When Elizabeth was sent to juvenile hall for breaking a window, Pat went to the city dog pound and let several dogs out. Then she sat on the police station steps, waiting to be sent to juvenile hall, too, so Elizabeth wouldn't be alone. Another time, they decided to run away together. "We got as far as Waco, Texas, then decided we'd rather be home, so we turned back," says Elizabeth.

Birth Parent Family Interview

Make copies of this form for every family member/friend who is going to be interviewed. Fill in every blank—if you don't know the answer use "unknown." Label answers that are known for certain with a star (*). Use this list as a basic guide and attach any questions of your own on the last page.

1. Exactly where did I give birth? _____

2. What was the name of the hospital? _____

3. Do we have a copy of my child's amended birth certificate? _____ Where is it? _____

4. Do we have a copy of my child's original birth certificate? _____ Where is it? _____

5. What were we told about the adoptive parents? _____

	Birth Mother	**Birth Father**
Names:		
Ages:		
Exact DOBs:		
Places of Birth:		
Nationalities:		
Education Levels:		
Religions:		
Military Service:		
Physical Descriptions:		
Other Children:		
Their Parents:		
Their Brothers/Sisters:		
Deaths in Family:		

Download a copy of this form at <http://reunite.myfamily.com/forms>.

Their friendship included both mischief and companionship. "We were tighter than sisters," Elizabeth says today. "Pat called me Yankee because I was from Massachusetts."

Elizabeth moved back to her native Massachusetts after two years. But she never forgot Pat. She named her daughter Patricia after her old friend. "I never had a friend that stayed in my mind like she has. I never stopped thinking of her," says Elizabeth.

Later in life, after she had married twice and was a grandmother, Elizabeth started to look for Pat. Her granddaughter searched the Internet for two years without success. Elizabeth bought a book about how to search for people. I became aware of Elizabeth's search, and decided to help her locate her old friend.

I called Elizabeth one day recently. It had been forty-seven years since she had last seen her friend Pat. "Do you have a paper and pencil handy?" I asked. "I have a phone number for you."

"I was beside myself," Elizabeth recalls. "I could hardly write the number down." She immediately called the phone number. "Is this Pat Murphy?" she asked when a woman answered. "Yes, this is Pat. Elizabeth? I got a letter from someone named Troy Dunn. It said someone was looking for me. As soon as I saw the word 'Yankee,' I knew it was you."

"Pat was stunned when I told her I had twenty grandchildren and twenty great-grandchildren," says Elizabeth. "Talking to her brought back wonderful memories." The two women discovered that they had each married twice, and each had children and grandchildren. They now talk on the phone every two days and send each other photos and messages over the Internet. Their dream is to meet again in person someday. And it was a relief to discover that each had gone on to lead a happy life. "Despite the fact that we were mischief-makers as girls, we both turned out okay," says Elizabeth today. She was surprised to discover that Pat had even worked for the police department for fifteen years.

"Before I heard from Elizabeth," Pat says, "I thought my life was more or less over. I had become depressed during my husband's illness and was ready to let life go by. Elizabeth brought me out of my sadness and I hope to hug her again before I die."

Most of the time, a search for an old friend is the easiest kind of search. You have the person's name as well as a lot of other information. There are literally hundreds of ways to find old friends and relatives. The easiest way to start this kind of search is simply to go back to the time and place where you

left off. For example, if you and your friend went to school together, the best place to begin is usually the institution you both attended.

When calling the school, ask where the records are kept for the years for which you are searching. Most schools keep only four to five years of records within reach. Older records are normally kept in a designated archive or records department. Once you determine the location of the records, simply call the office and tell the clerk that you would like help in reconnecting with an old friend. Give your friend's name and the years he or she attended the school. Once the clerk finds your friend's file, politely ask for his or her date of birth, parents' names, and any previous or updated addresses. Also ask if the employment of either parent is listed. Ask if the school has any record of where your friend may have gone.

If you know where a friend or relative graduated from college, another helpful source is the school's alumni association. Most colleges and universities spend a great deal of time and energy keeping track of their alumni, since a large part of their funding comes from donations.

Download a copy of the "Source and Document checklist" (see page 12) to list the information you know about your friend or relative. In this type of search, the information will most likely include name, age and date of birth, last known address, names of relatives/friends, school last attended, hobbies or interests, occupation, military service, and church attendance.

"Lost Family Member" Search

Again, the easiest rule for starting this kind of search is simply to go back to the time and place where you left off. For example, if you last saw your half-brother in Boca Raton, Florida, eight years ago, begin your search there. If you have his last known address there, neighbors could give you a clue to where he lives now. To get started on a search for a lost family member, use the Source and Document checklist and include everything you know about the person, no matter how insignificant. When you are looking for a relative, write down the following facts:

- **Name**. Be sure the spelling is correct, and if you're not sure, list all the possible spellings. If the person used a nickname, also be sure to list his or her legal or proper name, if known. A middle name or initial can be helpful, too, especially with a common last name.

- **Age and date of birth**. List the date of birth if you know it. If you're unsure, try to determine the approximate birthday based on the person's age and anything else you might remember.

- **Last known address**. What is the last address you have for this person? Again, old neighbors often have valuable clues.

- **Names of relatives/friends**. Do you know the name of your subject's father or mother? Siblings? These are people who, if located, might be able to tell you where the person is currently living. This may be the quickest way to locate someone.

- **School last attended**. The school or alumni group may have current information.

- **Occupation**. There are hundreds of occupations that require professional licensing, and all licenses are available to the public.

- **Possibly deceased**. If there's a chance the person is dead, you should verify that fact first. Death records are fairly easy to find, and doing so will save you time and energy. The Social Security Death Index on Ancestry.com is great place to start. (see pages 16 and 34 for more details on this valuable resource). Obituaries often provide the names of surviving friends and relatives.

- **Military service**. If your family member was in the military, see the military section on page 53.

- **Church attendance**. Did this person attend a particular church? Church records not only have helpful information, but they often note if the person requested that their membership be transferred to another church. A church will usually provide you with the forwarding church's address.

Lost Love Search

Each month, I receive thousands of calls and e-mails from people who are looking for a missing piece of their heart—a lost love! One might assume that the majority of these requests come from females, but the determined drive to find a lost love is motivated by hearts both male and female, young and old.

Often a search for a lost love is an attempt to find closure so life can go on without past memories interfering with a current or future relationship. Other lost loves seem more like "soul mates" who think of each other every day as years past, although they do not communicate. Still others have pleasant memories of their past relationship and play a "what if?" game in their minds. It's not unusual for a person to wonder, "What ever happened to…?" or "What would my life be like now if…?" Sometimes old loves have a permanent place in our hearts. Finding a lost love rarely results in the rekindling of an old flame, but it often provides peace of mind.

When she was in junior high, fourteen-year-old Sara Montgomery thought Rick Douglas just happened to have classes in the same halls she did. She never guessed that he arrived at school an hour early every day and posted himself in the foyer just hoping to catch a glimpse of her. Or that between classes, he ran as fast as he could to reach a point where he knew their paths would cross near the English and homemaking classrooms.

"The moment I saw Sara, I knew I was in love," says Rick, "although today my behavior might be called stalking." Both were extremely shy, and it was months before they actually talked. Rick continued to follow Sara in clandestine forays. He'd ride his bike past her house hoping to see her. He rode on her bus after school even though he lived in a different direction.

Eventually, Sara's best friend, Marlene, observed their attraction and began to play Cupid. She oversaw their conversations in the halls and school meditation chapel. Their friendship deepened into a relationship as they discovered mutual interests in bowling and music. "Rick has very expressive eyes. The way he looked at me caused 'that special feeling' and I wasn't interested in anyone else," Sara recalls. "Our common interests helped build the relationship, too. He would pop up next to me in the hall and ask questions like, 'What is the proper name for Handel's composition—is it *Messiah* or *The Messiah?*' A class picnic allowed them to be alone together for the first time. "We went for a ride in a rowboat—Rick didn't know I was afraid of deep water," Sara remembers.

Still, best-friend Marlene had to force shy Rick to ask Sara to the prom. Although outwardly everything went wrong on their prom date, from bad restaurant food to getting lost on the freeway, they still had their first kiss and Rick knew he wanted to spend time with Sara after high school ended. He asked if he could call her and they decided they wanted to remain friends no matter what.

Not long after, discord struck when they disagreed about two issues. Sara had always dreamed of becoming a nurse and had been a candy striper in high school. Along with her hopes of entering the medical field, she hoped to marry a doctor or professional man. Rick was headed for a new 70s career field—electronic engineering—that struck her as distinctly blue collar. ("I'll never live that misconception down today," Sara laughs.)

They also disagreed about the Vietnam War. Sara saw herself as possibly a Navy nurse and serving in the Vietnam conflict, while Rick was a confirmed conscientious objector.

"Though we continued to converse, Sara gradually let me know that this wasn't a relationship that would work past high school," says Rick, who continued to pursue her after she left for college. He'd take all of his change to a wooden phone booth at a nearby drugstore and talk to her as long as he could. Their last conversation took place when he called her dorm, and she told the house mother, "Just tell him I'm not here" without realizing that Rick was also on the phone line.

Both Sara and Rick each married and divorced other people in the ensuing thirty years. Through the years, neither forgot the other. Sara would never have guessed that Rick was both geographically and philosophically located in the last place she would look—in an Air Force engineering career on the West Coast. She called the *Sally Jessy Raphael* show in response to a request for people seeking lost loves.

"I broke up with the man of my dreams, and I want him back," Sara proclaimed. She never imagined that that same week, Rick was visiting back home.

"I planned to drive past her house to see if she might be in the front yard reading a book or standing on the stairs," says Rick. "Unfortunately, I forgot how to find her street." On the day he planned to visit her neighborhood he received a message on his answering machine. "Even if I hadn't been contacted, I planned to look for Sara in a week or two," says Rick.

The two were reunited on the *Sally Jessy Raphael* show in 1996. They spent that evening getting reacquainted. Their families were thrilled. "Before I could even say hi, his mom gave me a bone-crushing hug and said, 'It's about time,'" Sara recalls. Later, Sara's mother also hugged Rick saying, "It's been so long. I'm glad."

"Our families are ecstatic that we came together again and the love shared by my daughter and Rick is wonderful," says Sara. "We look into each other's eyes and the years just wash away."

Sara and Rick married in 1999. "I turned fifty on March 15, and he still has me blushing and feeling like that teenager he first fell in love with," says Sara. "Our reunion started a domino effect in which we have located six former classmates who were considered missing—including our 'Cupid' and Rick's best friend with whom we double-dated on prom night."

While in many ways searching for a lost love is much like searching for a missing friend or lost family member, the manner of inquiry and the method of making first contact is unique. Remember, your lost love may or may not have told his or her current significant other about the place you held in his or her past. It is imperative to respect and value the sanctity of home and family. Always maintain healthy and appropriate boundaries in your search for a former love.

As you look for your old flame, you will gather various bits of information from people like former employees, school secretaries, and even his or her family members.

In most cases it's best to keep the story of your past romance to yourself when you're trying to get information. The "lost love" angle only confuses things and may make people nervous, so keep it simple and proceed as though you are looking for an old friend. I've found that if you tell the whole story, people who are close to the individual you're seeking may tend to pass judgment on your motives. And if they judge you and your motives negatively, they may deny you the information you are requesting.

For example, a sister of your former love may choose not to tell you where her happily married brother is now living, for fear that you might interfere with his marriage. If, however, she considers you just an old friend, she will probably be more willing to pass along the information.

Military Personnel Search

The most common military search is initiated by a person looking for a missing father. It's also common for people to look for old military buddies with whom they've lost touch over the years. Locating someone who is or has been in the military is one of those rare cases where we can be grateful for government red tape. Active military personnel cannot make a move without a mountain of paperwork following them. Our government's system of veteran benefit programs makes locating former military personnel relatively simple.

If you are looking for a lost love, an old friend, a birth parent, or anyone else, find out, if you can, if that person was ever in the military. It truly is easier to track down someone who has been in the service.

Online Military Searches

The following links specifically address military resources

- **www.globemaster.de/faq/locator.html**—This is a large online information service for locating military personnel. After giving some general search information, this site lists each branch of the military and provides the contact information for each. It also includes links to other helpful websites.
- **www.thewall-usa.com/cgi-bin/mboard.cgi**—The homepage of this site <www.thewall-usa.com> lists all the names on the Vietnam Memorial in Washington, D.C. This section of the site features a message board that you can use to post "looking for information regarding…" queries.

Offline Military Searches

First, limited information from military personnel files is available to anyone under the Freedom of Information Act. This information typically includes name, rank/grade, duty status, date of rank/grade, service number, dependents, gross salary, geographic locations of duty assignments, military/civilian education level, awards and decorations, official photograph, city and state of last known residence, and date and place of induction, and discharge.

To obtain official records or specific information, send a copy of Standard Form 180: Request Pertaining to Military Records <http://www.archives.gov/facilities/mo/st_louis/military_personnel_records/ standard_form_180.html> to the National Personnel Records Center (NPRC). There is no charge to former service members or their next of kin; however, others may have to pay a small fee for research and photocopying. If you plan to take this route, be patient. Since the NPRC receives 200,000 letters and requests each month, a reply can take several months to receive. Send requests regarding military personnel to the first address and requests regarding civilians employed by the military to the second address.

National Personnel Records Center
Military Personnel Records
9700 Page Boulevard
St. Louis, MO
63132-5100

National Personnel Records Center—Civilian Records
111 Winnebago St.
St. Louis, MO 63118-4199
314-425-5722
Army: (314) 538-4122
Army (prior 1960): (314) 538-4144
Air Force: 314-538-4218
Navy, Marines, Coast Guard: (314) 538-4200

In addition to providing general information, the NPRC will also forward correspondence to veterans at their last known address. Normally, this service is reserved for situations considered "in the veteran's best interest." The NPRC will open your letter and read it. If the letter meets their requirements, they will forward it. You will not be informed of the outcome.

The Department of Veterans Affairs

The Department of Veterans Affairs will also forward letters to veterans of the armed services. Before sending a letter, contact your local library and ask for the address and telephone number of the nearest VA office, or call (800) 827-1000 for your closest VA regional office. Call that office and tell a counselor you wish to verify if a veteran is listed in their files before mailing any correspondence. Give the individual's full name, service number, social security number, and VA file number or claim number. If you do not have this information, the VA can sometimes still identify the right person from a date of birth, branch of service, or even the name alone if it is uncommon. If they find the individual, ask for his or her VA claim number and anything else they'll tell you. You will need the claim number later on, and any other information is always helpful.

If your regional office can't find the individual in their files, contact the VA insurance office in Philadelphia at the following address:

Department of Veterans Affairs
P.O. Box 13399
Philadelphia, PA 19101
(213) 842-2000

To have a letter forwarded, place your correspondence in an unsealed, stamped envelope *without* your return address. Put the veteran's name and VA claim number on the front of this envelope. Next, prepare a short fact sheet and request that the VA forward this letter to the individual. Tell them you were given the VA claim number by their regional office. Include all the information you know about the veteran to help make sure they identify the right person. Place all of this in a large envelope and mail it to the regional VA office you spoke with. If they cannot find the individual, they will return your letter to you. They will also inform you if the letter was undeliverable by the post office. In general, the VA is very cooperative in providing assistance in locating veterans.

If you know a veteran's full name, date of birth, and service number, it may be possible to obtain his or her Social Security number, if he or she applied for benefits after April 1973. For this information, contact:

Department of Veterans Affairs
VA Records Processing Center
P.O. Box 5020
St. Louis, MO 63115
(314) 538-2050

Call the above number to determine the amount of the nominal fee for this service. Enclose a check or money order for that amount, payable to the Department of Veterans Affairs. Request the veteran's claim number. If the veteran has applied for some type of VA benefit, Veterans Affairs will be able to provide you with a nine-digit claim number preceded by "C" or "XC" if the person is deceased. After April, 1973, this number is the same as the veteran's Social Security number.

Lost and Found

The Military's Worldwide Locator Offices

If you suspect that the person you are searching for is still in the military, each branch of the service maintains a worldwide locator office that will either forward a letter or provide you with the current military unit of assignment within the United States.

If you want a letter forwarded, place it in a sealed, stamped envelope. Put your name and return address in the upper left-hand corner. In the center of the envelope, put the full name of the individual, rank, and social security number (if known, but it's not absolutely necessary). On a separate sheet, list everything you know that may help the agency identify the person.

In a legal-size envelope, enclose the following: the fact sheet with all the identifying information you have, the letter you want forwarded, and a check for $3.50 made out to the United States Treasury. If you state on the fact sheet that you are a family member, a fee will not be charged. Be sure to include your return address on the outside of this envelope. Address it to the appropriate locator office listed below. Even though an attempt will be made, a reply cannot be guaranteed. If the person cannot be found, you will be notified.

If the person you are seeking cannot be located through traditional military record sources, or if you don't have his or her full name, use the strategies explained in this book to track the person down. But with a name, Social

---

Military Worldwide Locator Offices

Air Force
AFPC-MSIMDL
550 C Street W., Suite 50
Randolph AFB, TX 78150-4752
(210) 652-5774 or (210) 652-5775

Army
USAEREC
Indianapolis, IN 46249-5301
(317) 542-4211

Coast Guard
Personnel Commander CGPC-ADM-3
2100 2nd St. SW #1616
Washington, DC 20593-0001
(202) 267-1340

Marine Corps
HQMC-MMSB-10
2008 Elliot Rd. #20
Quantico, VA 22134-5030

Navy
Bureau of Navy Personnel
2 Navy Annex P-02116
Washington, DC 20370-0216
(703) 614-3155

Security number, and geographical information, you should be able to turn to the military records and find the person successfully.

Professional Searchers

It's surprising that most people choose professional searchers not because they can't search themselves, but more often because they don't have the time. Or sometimes the emotional investment is too close to the heart and raises issues from which the searcher has previously distanced himself. A searcher may wonder, "What if my birth mother doesn't want to talk to me?" Other searches do require the assistance of a professional because of their complexity.

If you choose to seek the services of a professional searcher, keep the following information in mind.

- The cost will vary. Prices for a professional search range from as low as $500 to as high as $4,000. If the fee is lower than $500, the searcher probably isn't doing anything you can't do yourself. If the amount is higher than two or three thousand dollars, the searcher is likely taking advantage of your willingness to pay.

- Beware of guarantees. If a searcher "guarantees" that he will find someone, it could mean that he is willing to break the law to do so, and if he is charged with a crime, there may be charges against you as well. Making a guarantee to find a missing person is like making a guarantee to find oil in your backyard—you might have to put it there yourself. Fees paid to a professional searcher are for services rendered, not results. The situation is comparable to paying a doctor to perform surgery. He is paid simply to do his best work; he has no idea how your body will react, or to what degree the surgery will be considered successful.

- To undertake a professional search, the searcher should be licensed as an investigator. Feel free to ask to see his or her license.

- Keep in mind that there are many people who are unlicensed and unregulated who set themselves up as investigators. They are often good-hearted people with an interest in helping others but who nevertheless have not been trained or licensed. They will often provide you with information without verifying that this is the actual person you are seeking.

• Because adoption searches are the most difficult to complete and so many people are seeking their birth families, many private investigators list "adoption searches" among the services they offer in their Yellow Pages listings. Keep in mind that private investigators are, again, like doctors in that they have different specialities. You probably wouldn't ask an ear, nose, and throat specialist to deliver your baby. Likewise, you probably would prefer to ask someone other than an insurance fraud investigator to search for your birth family. A licensed investigator should also be able to offer references from past successful adoption searches for you to contact.

After the Search

$\blacktriangledown$

The realization that you may have found the person you are looking for is an indescribable phenomenon. Somehow, the idea that you have reached the conclusion of your search validates all of the hope, longing, research, and efforts that you have made. At the moment you realize you may have achieved success, your initial impulse might be to instantly call the person you believe is the one you are seeking. In your excitement, however, you may risk jumping to conclusions or assumptions that may not be accurate.

In less sensitive searches, such as a military search or old friend search, you may feel free to phone the person and ask, "Are you the Brent Hall who attended East High School in 1971?" or "Are you the Allen Sorensen who served in the First Air Cavalry Division in Vietnam in 1972?

On the other hand, in a sensitive search, such as a lost love or adoption search, try to verify other variables in addition to the name match. Make efforts to determine whether other facts—such as age, race, and birth date—also meet the profile of the person you are seeking. One way to attempt to verify the person's identity is to do searches on one or more search engines, such as Google. The individual's website, employment or professional affiliations, and postings on other Internet sites may provide corroborating information.

The most direct way to determine whether such variables match is to make a "verification" phone call to determine whether more than one criterion matches your research. Because a "verification" phone call may become a "contact call" please also read the "contact call" section that follows before making your first phone call to the person who appears to match your search criteria.

If you have found a name and phone number, remember that the number could now be a working number for someone other than the person you want to reach. If you decide to make a verification phone call to locate an Ann Hansen, first ask, "Is this the Hansen residence?" If the answer is yes, you will at least know that the number still belongs to someone with the last name you are seeking.

Then, if your instincts tell you it's all right to proceed, say, "May I speak to Ann?" If the response is, "This is Ann," and it still feels appropriate to proceed, you might say something like, "I want to be sure I have the right person," and then offer one or two of the following reasons for your call: "I'm looking for an old friend," or "I'm doing some research relating to my family tree."

Then, it's more likely to be appropriate to ask for verifying information such as, "Hansen is a common name. Was your maiden name Walker?" or, "The Ann I'm looking for would be about forty-two years old." or, "In the family I'm trying to locate, there were two boys and a girl." Such questions could lead to a response that verifies that this is not the right person, such as "My maiden name wasn't Walker. It was Phillips," or, "That couldn't be me, I'm only thirty," or, "I don't have any brothers or sisters. I am an only child."

If you discover that the person you have called is not the person you are looking for, you could say, "It doesn't appear that I've found the right person, but, if I have more questions, would you mind if I called you back?" A request to call back if there are more questions will allow you to "resurface," if you should discover that a piece of your initial information or research is incorrect or incomplete. In that case, additional research may indicate that this person is once again the possible object of your search.

Of course, once you begin asking questions, the other party is likely to become curious, too. It's important to wait to reveal the purpose of your call until you have created a receptive atmosphere. Read the next section about contact calls, which suggests ways to proceed if you feel you have verified that you have found the right person.

Contact Call

After you feel relatively certain—hopefully by confirming several facts—that you have found the person you are seeking, the next step is to make the contact call. This is the most important telephone call of your search. It can be the most climactic moment of the entire reunion experience. This single phone call answers the two basic questions of reunion. "Is she alive?" and "Does she want to meet me?" or "Does he want to see me again?" The contact call is actually the "pre-reunion" before you meet in person, and can shape the comfort level of the entire reunion experience that follows.

Choosing a Good Time to Call

If you don't re-enter your friend or loved one's life at the proper pace, you can ruin a great reunion experience. Although it isn't easy to determine the most opportune time to call someone that you've never met, there are some typically less-convenient times to avoid.

Don't call between 5:00 and 6:00 P.M.—a common dinner time. Do not call first thing in the morning, when the person you are trying to reach is likely either preparing to leave for work or helping children get ready for school. During these two times—the dinner hour and the morning rush—the person you want to call is also more likely to be surrounded by family members and not in a position to enjoy an important—and possibly intense—conversation.

In a sensitive search—a lost love or adoption search—try to call once during the middle of the day. If there is no answer, make an attempt at an evening call after the dinner hour—between 7:00 and 9:00 P.M. If you encounter an answering machine, don't reveal the purpose of the call by saying, "It's about the baby she gave up for adoption," or "I'm his old girlfriend." Another family member may answer the phone and ask, "May I tell him what this is regarding?" In this case, you may want to reply, "No, thank you. I'll just call later." If the person who answers the phone continues to press you for an explanation, consider saying, "I'm working on personal family research." While this answer may "feel" deceptive, it's important to remember that you owe the person you are seeking respect and privacy.

In contacting someone from the past, never assume that the other person shares the same degree of enthusiasm you have. As you re-enter this person's life, you've been preparing yourself—possibly for weeks, months, or years—while the person you seek has no idea that the next phone call or letter will bring a greeting from an old love or the first word from a son or daughter she surrendered for adoption years ago. Respect this person's privacy by remembering that he or she may or may not have told those currently in his or her life about you. As a searcher, it is not your place to disclose to a spouse or child a relationship that the person you are seeking has kept secret.

It's much more effective to make one or more additional calls until you reach the person. Remember, too, that if you are excited and call repeatedly during a single day, the person could return home to find ten calls from an unfamiliar number on the caller I.D.—and that could make him or her nervous. Even if you happen to acquire a work number for the person you are seeking, don't call her at work to drop what could be an emotional bombshell. Wait until you find the person you are seeking at home, again during an after-dinner hour between 7:00 and 9:00 P.M.

What to Say

Take a deep breath and move into the contact call with calmness and control. You might want to consider preparing a list of questions. Remember that your method of re-entry into someone's life has everything to do with your long-term relationship with that person.

Once you are actually speaking with the person you have searched for, don't immediately dive into the purpose of the call. For example, your birth mother's husband—who she has never told about you—could be standing right beside her. Or possibly, she's told her husband but not her son, who is also sitting at the kitchen table. If this happens, she feels she is left no option but to say, "I'm sorry. I'm not the person you are looking for." Or, "I'm sorry, you have the wrong number," before hanging up. And her first feelings toward you may be anger and frustration.

When the person you are seeking comes to the phone, say something like, "This is Troy Dunn. I'm working on some family history. Is this a good time to talk?"

It's true that the person you are seeking may also have anticipated this reunion for thirty years, but it's still best to proceed very slowly and ease him or her into the possibility of connection. And if he or she states that the time of your first call isn't convenient, say, "I'm sorry. When is a better time for me to call you back?" Maybe the next morning or next evening really would be a more convenient time.

When you eventually reach the person you are seeking at a convenient time for both of you, begin to gently lay out the details that will allow her to draw the conclusion of your connection. Start by saying something like, "My name is Troy Dunn. I was born in Los Angeles, California. My date of birth is June 14, 1970." While you slowly recite the facts, this woman is bringing herself to the reality of what is about to be said long before you point out the specifics of how you are connected. At any point in your recitation of the facts, she may jump in and say, "Oh, my gosh. I've been looking for you."

Until she responds, simply continue moving forward with a recitation of the facts that are part of your research. "I've written to the state of California and received a copy of my original birth certificate, which says that my birth mother's name is Carolyn Edwards." Hopefully, she will have responded affirmatively by now, but if not, you might conclude by saying, "Based on all the information I've discovered, my search leads me to believe that you might be my biological mother." Again, hopefully, she will have jumped into the conversation by now.

Although this gentle, gradual approach increases the odds of a positive response, your birth mother might be afraid at this point. She might think you'll blow her cover or ruin her reputation at church or somehow interfere negatively in her life. If she doesn't respond affirmatively after you've made the conclusive statement, continue to reassure her of your confidentiality in a calm, soothing tone. Say something like, "I want you to know that this is not something I've discussed with anyone else in your family. I have no intention of telling anyone in your family. I am just looking for closure for myself. I'd be very grateful for some family or medical information."

If you are seeking a long-lost relative who broke off contact with the family on purpose—a sibling who ran away or an aunt who cleared out after a family crisis—it's crucial that you take care when making a contact call. Whether you re-establish contact by phone or by letter, help this person feel safe. Give him or her the ability to choose whether to speak with you, as well as when or how. It is sometimes helpful to let the person know that it doesn't have to be a "package deal." You'll respect her wishes if she still doesn't want to talk to a particular family member. You won't bring the entire clan knocking at her door. Take it one step at a time and be caring and sensitive to the dynamics of the situation.

Because I believe deeply in the value and joy of family, I think that finding missing family members is the most satisfying search of all.

Third-person Contact Call

If you sense that it will be hard for you to present yourself in the calm, controlled way described above, consider sharing this book and the techniques it discusses with a third person—a willing friend or other intermediary—who will then make the contact call for you. If you feel sure that you will cry or cannot maintain a level head, feel free to ask someone else to make this important call on your behalf. Ask this person to read all of the sections included here—such as the one about choosing an opportune time—so that he or she can make the call for you.

The Possibility of Rejection

Most birth parents, lost loves, and people who are sought by searchers like you are happy that someone remembers them and wants to reconnect. They are also willing to pursue the possibility of connection, even if it's just in a single meeting. But in a very small minority of adoption contact calls, the result is rejection. Most adoptees feel it is worth the risk of rejection to find out the truth.

There are two types of rejection, a hard rejection and a soft rejection. In an instance of soft rejection, the birth mother is so stunned by the magnitude of this first phone call, that she needs time to process the reality of the situation. While she might say, "I can't talk to you now," or "I don't think I'm the person you're looking for," the reality is that she hasn't given any thought to a reunion taking place, and needs to consider this possibility for a few hours or a few days to get past the shock. Once she comes to terms with the situation, her thoughts will be something like, "Yes, I do want to know more about my birth son. Is he married? Is he healthy?"

Now she is the one who has questions, and the situation turns around and becomes a positive possibility within days.

In a very few instances, the result of the contact call is a "hard" rejection, in which the birth mother or lost love says something like "I really want nothing to do with this. Please don't call me again." If this happens, reassure the person that you will keep the phone call confidential. In the case of an adoption, say something like, "I have no intention of discussing this with anyone in your family, but I would be really grateful for some medical information." If this is your birth mother and you sense this is definitely the last phone conversation the two of you will exchange, see if she will allow you to seek medical information through the questions you have prepared. Despite the sense of rejection you may feel, gently insist that she take down your name and phone number. Say, "If you will take down my contact information, I will not bother you again." Ask her to read the information back to you, so you know that the information has been written down.

Is there a way to move past such a rejection? I have heard of people who have stalked a lost love or birth parent, or sent them tons of letters that end up in the hands of other family members. I believe that it is imperative to respect a person's wishes if he or she truly does not wish to pursue a reunion.

Contacting Siblings of the Target Person

If your birth parent does not wish to seek a reunion, should you contact siblings or other family members? If you experience a hard rejection, the temptation might be to simply pick up the phone and call other family members. The moment you make such a call, you burn whatever bridge might remain with your birth mother because you have taken her secret and exposed it to other family members. After hearing from you, the sibling's first inclination will be to call your birth mother and say, "Is this true, Mom? You never mentioned having a son. Do I have a brother?"

The likely result of such a call is that your sibling will view you as an intruder who is "hurting Mom."

On the other hand, if you firmly feel that there will be no further contact with your birth mother, and there is zero chance of a reunion, you may feel that contact with a sibling will be the only source of contact between you and your birth family.

If you feel this way, wait a year. In the course of twelve months following the initial contact call, your birth parent will live through many experiences that may cause her to reconsider the possibility of a reunion. Events such as Christmas, Mother's Day, and the anniversary of the day she gave birth to you may influence her to desire some sense of connection. But if she doesn't reconsider within the year, it's likely she won't change her mind. And if you find that you still want a connection with your birth family, consider making a contact call to your sibling, using the same calm technique as when you called your birth mother.

If you do speak with another family member, avoid discussing your contact call experience with your birth mother.

"Lost Love" Contact Call

In the case of a lost love contact call, remember that he or she may not have told anyone about you. Rather than beginning with a romantic statement such as "I never stopped thinking of you, and I love you from the bottom of my heart," I would begin with the more casual, "I don't know if you remember me or not, but...." The response to this statement will likely give a clue to whether your lost love has also been thinking of you. If someone says, "Yes, I vaguely remember," it's still possible that they are thinking of you. But if you give your name and the response is, "Are you kidding? I think of you all the time," you know things are looking good.

The Reunion

Your search is complete, you've made your contact call, and now you are about to reach your goal—meeting in person. Where should the actual reunion take place? You have three options—your place, their place, or a neutral place.

How open is this reunion situation? If your birth mother hasn't told anyone in her family, you won't be going to her house. If your old army buddy can't afford a plane ticket right now, he won't be visiting your home.

If this is an out-in-the-open situation, you might consider having the reunion at your home. This way, your birth mother can visit your house, see all your scrapbooks, meet your friends, and have a wonderful time. The next time, you can visit her house, see all her scrapbooks, and what her life is like.

If you sense that the reunion will be sensitive in some way, choose a neutral location. Meeting for a meal at a restaurant is a safe choice, because a meal has a definite beginning and ending. If you find yourself stuck in an awkward situation, it's perfectly acceptable to ask the waitress to bring the check, and say that you need to leave after the meal is over. On the other hand, if you meet for a meal and find that you'd like to extend your reunion a bit longer, it's perfectly acceptable to say something like, "Now that we're through here, let's take a walk down by the park."

For a lost-love reunion meeting, lunch at a restaurant is a more comfortable choice than a candlelight dinner at 7 P.M. A casual lunch is a good way to avoid looking as if you are coming back into the relationship too fast or too soon.

Bringing scrapbooks or photos will help you break the ice at a first meeting. Looking through old photo albums gives you something to occupy your hands and fills the void of "What should we talk about?" Bringing a simple gift to commemorate the significance of the occasion is also appropriate. You might also consider bringing along a camera and asking the waitress to take your picture. After all, in some cases, this lunch meeting may be the only time you are together in person.

This should be a small gathering with just you and this one other person. You might be tempted to bring along your best friend for moral support. Or, in an adoption reunion, you might feel inclined to invite your adoptive mother to meet your birth mother. After all, you love her, you're proud of her, and you don't want her to be hurt. But, bringing along other people dilutes the moment of first reunion. Instead of being able to focus all your energy on experiencing the emotions of the meeting, you will feel the need to include your adoptive mother in each moment. A first meeting works best if only the two key players are involved. If you would still like your adoptive and birth mothers to meet, plan a second meeting.

After the Reunion

Your reunion will likely bring you validation, healing, and a sense of closure. It will also be a positive experience that will help you find answers and truth. Will you continue to see each other? Or will you just meet one time?

If you are lost loves, whether or not you remain in contact depends on your current situation. It's unlikely, yet possible, that you will rekindle your relationship. It's far more likely that you will achieve closure and peace of mind, and possibly a renewed friendship.

If you are old friends who have made the effort to find each other years later, you will probably keep in touch for the rest of your lives. If you

are old military buddies, you are also likely to remain in contact.

Ninety percent of adoption reunions have positive results in that the searcher's questions are answered. Adoption reunions often begin with a "honeymoon period" where the excitement is intense and the reality of actually meeting is euphoric. It's like taking a vacation to a foreign city. When you first arrive at your new destination, everything seems perfect. You like everything about the place. But as time passes, you are reminded that this isn't like your hometown. Remember, an adoption reunion is unique. One day, you and your birth family are strangers. The next day, you are relatives. You have genetics in common, but no shared history.

Such a small number of shared memories often does not sustain the intense emotion of the initial reunion and may be followed by a cooling-off period that dictates the pace of the future relationship. Maybe your birth mother wants to get together for Christmas, to go on shared vacations, and to e-mail daily. On the other hand, maybe a phone call or e-mail once a week feels like the right amount of contact for you. In post reunion, the person who has the lesser enthusiasm of the two is the one who sets the pace. The person who has greater enthusiasm is happy to sustain the relationship and will usually accept the terms of the one whose feelings are less enthusiastic.

Sometimes the amount of future interaction relates to logistics more than enthusiasm. Maybe one of you lives a much more complicated life than the other. Maybe that person travels for business and only has access to e-mail once a week. Or maybe the fact that you live a thousand miles away leads to fewer in-person meetings. No matter what the future brings, you will find that the process of reunion completes you. As the relationship continues, there are ups and downs, and sometimes one party wants a closer relationship than the other.

In adoption reunions, the reunited adoptee sometimes asks, "What should I call my birth mother?" The fact is, you already have a mom, the woman who raised you. You may choose to call your birth mother by her first name. Or you may call her "Mom," too, particularly if you establish a close relationship. While the titles of "mother" and "father" don't always work in an adoption reunion situation, the outcome is most often a rich, meaningful friendship. How can anyone have too many people who care about him?

Most adoptees who request a search are seeking their own identities rather than a new set of parents. Adoptive parents sometimes worry that their children want to find a new mom and dad, which is not true. After the search, your relationship with your adoptive parents may actually be strengthened.

You may find that meeting a birth relative is like acquiring a relative later in life—say a brother-in-law or a step-parent by marriage. While you'll never share childhood memories, there's an undeniable bond and a sense of future closeness. In ways, you may feel like you've always known each other. As time passes, you may continue to share conversations, recipes, Christmas cards, and an occasional visit.

Staying in Touch

After your reunion, it's exciting to be able to stay in touch with the person or people you've wanted to meet for so long. You will likely write more often than you talk, and share a conversation more often than a visit. There may be many miles between you, and it's a good possibility that you will want to communicate more often than you are able to travel to be together.

Happily, there are many ways to keep the lines of communication open to reinforce the new relationship. E-mail is a simple and convenient way to touch base on a regular basis. Exchanging videos of family events is another way to share special moments when you are miles apart. Within the video you might even speak directly to the person to whom you will send it. For example, a mom might say, "Here we are at Brittany's birthday party. Everyone wave to Aunt Janice."

Establish a Family Website

MyFamily.com websites are an easy, inexpensive, and accessible way for both newly reunited and traditional families to remain in contact. After creating a MyFamily.com website, you can share photos of your children, your favorite chocolate chip cookie recipe, holiday memories, greetings on special occasions, family information, photos, and jokes.

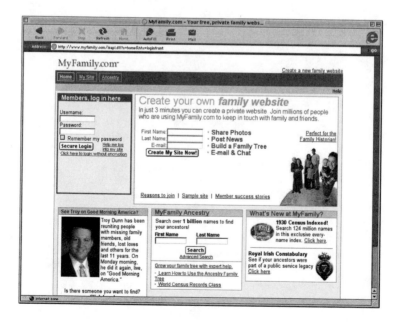

Lost and Found

A reunion is a unique and paradoxical experience. You will find yourself forever changed—yet even more secure in your own identity. Questions have been answered. A milestone has been reached. You have acquired self-knowledge along with an increased understanding of the person you were seeking. There is a feeling of completion. You are now able to go on to the next quest in your life, whatever it may be.

Adoption Websites

Adoption Crossroads
www.adoptioncrossroads.org

American Adoption Congress
www.americanadoptioncongress.org

About Adoption - Resources on Adoption
http://adoption.about.com

Adoption Network Cleveland
www.adoptionnetwork.org

Adoption Forum, Pennsylvania
www.adoptionforum.org

Adoption Network
www.adoption.org

Bastard Nation
www.bastardnation.org

Child Welfare League of America
www.cwla.org

Concerned United Birthparents
www.cubirthparents.org

Dave Thomas Foundation
www.davethomasfoundationforadoption.org

Eagle for Georgians
http://geocities.com/kisnet/eagleforgeorgians

Evan B. Donaldson Adoption Institute
www.adoptioninstitute.org

Information on Access to Adoption Records
www.whiteoakfoundation.org/mappage.htm

Insight: Open Adoption Resources and Support
www.openadoptioninsight.org

International Soundex Reunion Registry
www.isrr.net

National Adoption Center
www.nationaladoptioncenter.org

National Adoption Information Clearinghouse
www.calib.com/naic

New York State Citizens' Coalition for Children
www.nysccc.org

North Carolina Center for Adoption Education
www.adoptioneducationcenter.homestead.com/indexA.html

North American Council on Adoptable Children
www.nacac.org

Open Adoption Organization
www.openadoption.org

Oregon Adoption Rights Association
www.oara.org

National Listing of Adoption Search and Support Groups
www.paadoptionreunionregistry.org/BluePage.htm

Reunion Registry
http://www.reunionregistry.com/

Tapestry Books
www.tapestrybooks.com

Texas Coalition for Adoption Resources and Education
www.txcare.org

The Little Prince
www.thelittleprince.org

Universal Declaration of Human Rights
www.udhr.org

About the Author

*T*roy Dunn pioneered his system of locating lost family and friends back in 1990 while trying to assist his own family in locating biological relatives. Shortly thereafter, at the age of twenty-three, Dunn founded an organization whose sole purpose was to patch the world back together, one family at a time. This organization eventually reached across all fifty states and thirty-two countries, and today is responsible for reuniting thousands of families worldwide. Dunn has been featured hundreds of times on national television where he reunites people in front of millions of viewers. This national exposure got the attention of the executives at MyFamily.com, Inc. and, in the fall of 2002, Dunn and his organization joined the team at MyFamily.com as the in-house search and reunion experts. Dunn continues to be seen by millions of television viewers as he makes reunion dreams come true. Dunn resides in Florida with his wife of fifteen years (high school sweetheart) and their six children.

10/04

MyFamily.com Can Reunite You with Loved Ones!

If you have always wanted to reunite with a long-lost friend or family member, what are you waiting for?

MyFamily.com is creating ways for you to find and reunite with the people you care about—family members, old friends, military buddies, lost loves, and more!

Take two minutes right now and tell us your story! Fill out the quick form located at <http://reunite.myfamily.com/tv> and tell us your story. Who knows, you may be the next success story Troy Dunn highlights on national television.

SOCIAL SCIENCES DEPARTMENT
BIRMINGHAM PUBLIC LIBRARY
2100 PARK PLACE
BIRMINGHAM, ALABAMA 35203

MyFamily.com.

OCT 1 9 2004